Defining
MOMENTS

Martin Luther
KING, Jr.

I Have a Dream!

by Jacqueline A. Ball

CONSULTANT
Dr. Erica R. Armstrong
Assistant Professor of History
University of Delaware

BEARPORT
PUBLISHING COMPANY, INC.
New York, New York

Credits
Cover, © Flip Schulke/CORBIS; Title page, AP/Wide World Photos; 4, Hulton
Archive/Getty Images; 5, AP/Wide World Photos; 6–7 (both), The Granger
Collection, New York; 8, Library of Congress Prints and Photographs Division
Washington, DC; 9, The Granger Collection, New York; 10, CSU Archives
Courtesy Everett Collection; 11, AP/Wide World Photos; 12, Courtesy Crozer-
Chester Medical Center, Upland, Pa.; 13, The Granger Collection, New York;
14, Don Cravens/Time Life Pictures/Getty Images; 15, Grey Villet/Time Life
Pictures/Getty Images; 16, AP/Wide World Photos; 17, CSU Archives Courtesy
Everett Collection; 18–19 (both), AP/Wide World Photos/Bill Hudson; 20, Hulton
Archive/Getty Images; 21, Library of Congress Prints and Photographs Division
Washington, DC; 22–23 (both), AP/Wide World Photos; 24, © Bettmann/CORBIS;
25, Lynn Pelham/Time Life Pictures/Getty Images; 26, AP/Wide World Photos/
Elaine Thompson; 27, AP/Wide World Photos.

Editorial development by Judy Nayer
Design by Fabia Wargin; Production by Luis Leon; Image Research by Jennifer Bright

Library of Congress Cataloging-in-Publication Data
Ball, Jacqueline A.
  Martin Luther King, Jr. : I have a dream! / by Jacqueline A. Ball.
      p. cm. — (Defining moments)
  Includes bibliographical references and index.
  ISBN 1-59716-077-6 (library binding) — ISBN 1-59716-114-4 (pbk.)
  1. King, Martin Luther, Jr., 1929–1968—Juvenile literature. 2. African
Americans—Biography—Juvenile literature. 3. Civil rights workers—United
States—Biography—Juvenile literature. 4. Baptists—United States—Clergy—
Biography—Juvenile literature. 5. African Americans—Civil rights—History—
20th century—Juvenile literature. I. Title. II. Series: Defining moments (New York,
N.Y.)

E185.97.K5B356 2006
323'.092—dc22

2005005331

For more information, write to Bearport Publishing Company, Inc.,
101 Fifth Avenue, Suite 6R, New York, New York 10003.
Printed in the United States of America.

2 3 4 5 6 7 8 9 10

Table of Contents

A Great Shout for Freedom

The African-American man looked down the stone steps. Behind him was a statue of Abraham Lincoln. Below him was a sea of faces. The faces were young and old, black and white.

The March on Washington for Jobs and Freedom was the biggest **civil rights** march in American history.

Martin Luther King, Jr.

People had come to Washington, D.C., from all over America. They came because they loved freedom. They came because they believed in civil rights. They came to hear this man speak.

His voice was magic. His words could fill sad hearts with hope. America needed hope now more than ever.

It was August 28, 1963.

"I have a dream!" shouted the Reverend Dr. Martin Luther King, Jr.

For Whites Only

Dr. King's dream was of freedom. Millions of African Americans were living in a nightmare.

In some states, black children couldn't go to school with white children. The schools for whites were newer and better. The best hotels, theaters, and restaurants were for whites only. A black person couldn't get as good a job as someone who was white, or even vote in some places.

In the South and in some other states, black people couldn't even use the same drinking fountains as whites.

Many places, like this store, were closed to black people. Other places had separate entrances for whites and blacks.

Separating people by **race** was called **segregation**. Dr. King had worked hard to get segregation laws changed. His work was dangerous. People who fought segregation laws had been arrested. Some had been beaten.

In 1963, some black people were arrested for simply standing in a ticket line at a whites-only theater.

Back to the South

Government leaders feared there would be trouble at the March on Washington. Black people and white people seemed to be at war. In many places, it felt like the country was ready to explode.

Almost 250,000 people came to the March on Washington.

The March on Washington took place 100 years after President Abraham Lincoln began to make slavery **illegal**.

*President
Abraham Lincoln*

Dr. King was thankful that nothing bad happened at the march. He hated violence. He **preached** that love could **overcome** anything. He told people to demand their rights but to love their enemies.

After the speech, Dr. King headed back to the South. He knew it was a dangerous place for him, but he had important work to do. His wife and four children were there, too. The South had always been his home.

Martin's Childhood

Martin Luther King, Jr., was born on January 15, 1929, in Atlanta, Georgia. He had an older sister and a younger brother. His family called him M. L.

(Back row, from left) Martin's mother, Alberta King; his father, Martin Luther King, Sr.; and his grandmother, Jennie Williams. (Front row, from left) Martin's brother, Alfred Daniel; his sister, Christine; and Martin.

Martin grew up in this house in Atlanta, Georgia. Today the house is a museum.

Martin's father and grandfather were **ministers**. Martin heard them preach about love in church, but he didn't always see love around Atlanta. Once a white woman slapped him in a store. When Martin was six years old, he was told he couldn't play with two of his friends anymore. It was because he was black and they were white. Martin knew this type of treatment was wrong.

First Taste of Freedom

Martin was an excellent student. He graduated from high school when he was only 15 years old.

The summer after his graduation, Martin worked up North on a tobacco farm in Connecticut. There were no segregation laws there. He could use public bathrooms. He could eat in any restaurant. The freedom amazed him. He was more convinced than ever that segregation had to end in the South.

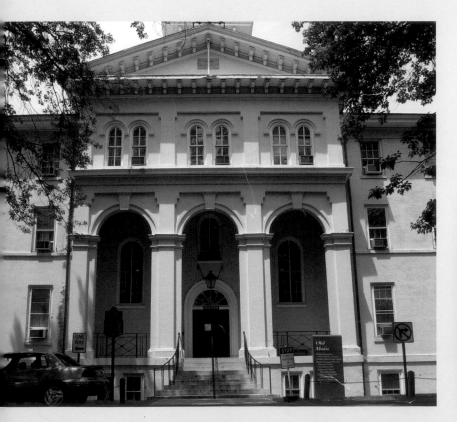

Martin studied to be a minister at Crozer Theological Seminary in Chester, Pennsylvania.

Some Northerners treated blacks unfairly, too. White **landlords** in Boston wouldn't rent Martin a room because he was black.

Martin decided to become a preacher so he could help this cause. After college he became head of a church in Montgomery, Alabama. He and his new wife, Coretta, moved there in 1954.

Martin met Coretta Scott when he was at Boston University, where he became a Doctor of Theology.

"Don't Ride the Bus!"

Montgomery's city buses were segregated. Black people had to sit in the back. White people sat up front. Blacks had to give their seats to whites if the bus was crowded.

On December 1, 1955, a black woman named Rosa Parks refused to give up her seat. Mrs. Parks was arrested.

Dr. King discusses with Rosa Parks (center) and others how to stop segregation on buses.

Dr. King and other church leaders decided it was time to challenge the laws. They asked all black people not to ride the bus until the law was changed.

The bus **boycott** lasted over a year. Finally, the law was changed. Dr. King had his first big victory.

Dr. King once stood for hours on an interstate bus while white people sat. It made him very angry.

During the bus boycott, black people walked or formed carpools to get to work.

Bombs and Death Threats

Many white people in Montgomery were furious. They didn't like sharing their seats with black people. They didn't like giving up their special rights. Also, the boycott had been bad for business. Bus companies lost thousands of dollars.

Many people blamed the boycott's leader, Martin Luther King, Jr. They wanted to get even with him.

Martin Luther King, Jr. (second row, left) rides Montgomery's first desegregated bus on December 21, 1956.

Montgomery police put Dr. King in jail because of a traffic ticket. The real reason for his arrest was the bus boycott.

Police made up reasons to arrest Dr. King. Segregationists bombed his house. The phone rang night and day with death **threats**. Dr. King, however, would not back down. In fact, he started traveling to other places to lead more **protests**.

The Children's Crusade

Dr. King went to Birmingham, Alabama, in April 1963. He was there to lead a march for better jobs. Thousands of people joined him. Many of them were children and teenagers. Some people called this protest the Children's Crusade.

The police used terrible force to stop the marchers. They sprayed them with high-pressure fire hoses. They beat them with clubs. They used fierce attack dogs.

The water pressure in the hoses was so strong it ripped bark off trees.

Protestors sat on the sidewalk in Birmingham as they were sprayed with hoses.

Dr. King taught protestors never to fight back, even when they were attacked. He said, "We must meet hate with love."

The protest lasted a month. TV stations sent reporters and camera crews. Every night Americans watched Birmingham police attack and arrest peaceful black adults and children. Now everyone knew how black people suffered in the South.

Just the Right Words

After the Children's Crusade, laws in Birmingham changed. Blacks could get better jobs. Dr. King had victories in other states, too.

"I have a dream that my four little children will one day live in a nation where they will not be judged by the color of their skin but by the content of their character. I have a dream today!"   —M. L. King, Jr.

Some black people, however, didn't think things were changing fast enough. They didn't agree with Dr. King's peaceful ways. They wanted to strike back at white people. At the same time, angry white **mobs** were attacking blacks.

When Dr. King planned the March on Washington, he knew he needed just the right words to bring everyone together. The words "I have a dream" came to him. On August 28, 1963, Dr. King spoke them straight from his heart.

You can read Dr. King's "I Have a Dream" speech at www.usconstitution.net/dream.html.

Blacks and whites rejoiced at Dr. King's message of hope.

Evil in Birmingham

In Washington, the huge crowd clapped and cheered. Blacks and whites cried and hugged each other. They waved signs saying "Free in '63!"

Dr. King (center) at the March on Washington, August 28, 1963

The blast was so strong it damaged cars outside the church.

However, that happy day was quickly followed by a sad one. On September 15, a church was bombed in Birmingham. Four black girls were killed. Many more people were hurt. Segregationists had planted the **dynamite**. They were getting even for the protest Dr. King had led in April.

Dr. King spoke at the funeral of three of the girls. He was horrified and sad. Still, he hoped that somehow good would come out of this terrible evil.

A Final Tragedy

Some good did come out of the bombing. Government leaders now knew tough laws were needed to protect black people. In 1964, **Congress** passed the Civil Rights Act. This law made it illegal to treat people differently because of their skin color.

Dr. King was praised everywhere for his brave work. However, some white people still hated him and everything he stood for.

In April 1968, Dr. King went to Memphis, Tennessee. He was there to help black garbage workers get better pay. During a break from a meeting, Dr. King went outside. He was shot to death by a white **racist**.

President Johnson shakes hands with Dr. King at the signing of the Civil Rights Act on July 2, 1964.

Fifty thousand people attended Dr. King's funeral in Atlanta, Georgia, on April 9, 1968.

"He Made
Our Nation Better"

The Reverend Dr. Martin Luther King, Jr., was not just a hero to black Americans. He was a hero to people of all colors, all over the world. He worked his whole life to make his dream of freedom come true for everyone. He never gave up believing that love could overcome hatred.

Martin Luther King, Jr., Day was made a national holiday in 1986. It is celebrated the third Monday in January.

Towns and cities all over the United States have parades to celebrate Martin Luther King, Jr., Day.

Martin Luther King, Jr., was a hero to his family, too. His wife, Coretta Scott King, has carried on his fight for equal rights.

In 1977, nine years after he died, Dr. King was given the Presidential Medal of Honor. On the medal are these words: "He helped us overcome our **ignorance** of each other. He made our nation stronger because he made it better."

Just the Facts

■ Martin and Coretta had four children: Yolanda, Martin Luther King the Third, Bernice, and Dexter.

■ Segregation laws were known as Jim Crow laws. Until the 1960s, these laws kept blacks and whites separate in many places such as schools and restaurants.

Timeline

Here are some important events in Dr. Martin Luther King, Jr.'s adult life and in the civil rights movement.

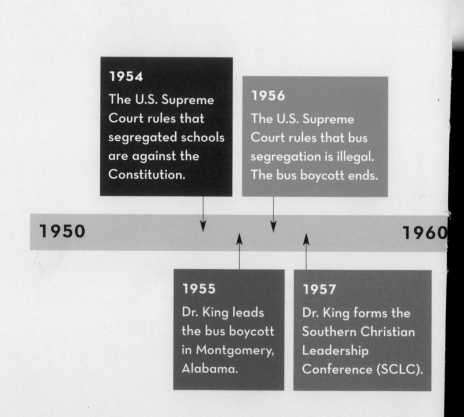

1954
The U.S. Supreme Court rules that segregated schools are against the Constitution.

1956
The U.S. Supreme Court rules that bus segregation is illegal. The bus boycott ends.

1950

1960

1955
Dr. King leads the bus boycott in Montgomery, Alabama.

1957
Dr. King forms the Southern Christian Leadership Conference (SCLC).

■ Dr. King preached at the same church as his father and grandfather in Atlanta, Georgia. It was called Ebenezer Baptist Church.

■ Dr. King started a group of Southern black ministers called the Southern Christian Leadership Conference (SCLC). This group was very important in ending segregation laws in the South.

■ In December 1964, when he was 35 years old, Dr. Martin Luther King, Jr., received the Nobel Peace Prize.

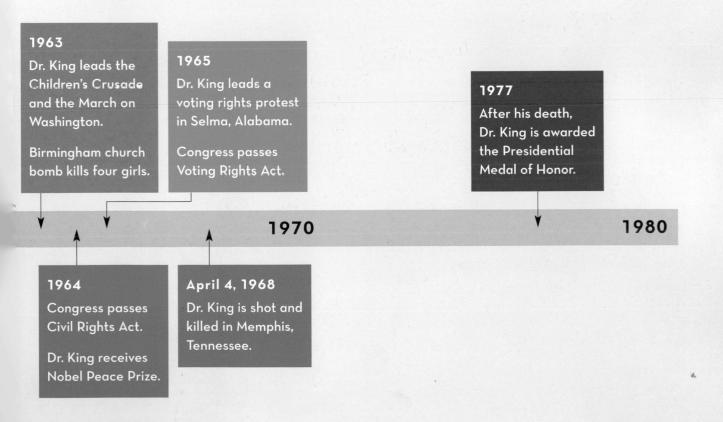

1963
Dr. King leads the Children's Crusade and the March on Washington.

Birmingham church bomb kills four girls.

1965
Dr. King leads a voting rights protest in Selma, Alabama.

Congress passes Voting Rights Act.

1977
After his death, Dr. King is awarded the Presidential Medal of Honor.

1970

1980

1964
Congress passes Civil Rights Act.

Dr. King receives Nobel Peace Prize.

April 4, 1968
Dr. King is shot and killed in Memphis, Tennessee.

Glossary

boycott (BOI-kot) the act of refusing to buy or use something in order to make a protest

civil rights (SIV-il RITES) in the United States, the certain rights people have under the law, such as the right to vote and the right to equal, fair treatment

Congress (KONG-griss) the branch of the U.S. government that makes laws

dynamite (DYE-nuh-mite) something that explodes

ignorance (IG-nur-uhns) lack of education or information

illegal (i-LEE-guhl) against the law

landlords (LAND-*lordz*) people who own and rent out apartments, rooms, or other buildings or land

ministers (MIN-uh-sturz) people who lead religious services in a church

mobs (MOBZ) large crowds of angry people

overcome (*oh*-vur-KUHM) to defeat or get over or past something, such as a feeling or a problem

preached (PREECHD) gave a religious talk to people, especially to teach something

protests (PROH-tests) demonstrations against something

race (RAYSS) one of the major groups of people in the world sharing certain physical features, such as skin color

racist (RAY-sist) someone who treats people unfairly or cruelly because of their race

segregation (seg-ruh-GAY-shuhn) the practice of keeping people separated by group, especially by race

threats (THRETS) warnings that punishment or harm will happen

Bibliography

Bullard, Sara. *Free at Last: A History of the Civil Rights Movement and Those Who Died in the Struggle.* New York: Oxford University Press (1994).

Gates, Henry Louis, Jr., and Evelyn Brooks Higginbotham, eds. *African American Lives.* New York: Oxford University Press (2004).

King, Martin Luther, Jr. *The Autobiography of Martin Luther King, Jr.* Edited by Clayborne Carson. New York: Warner Books (1998).

Oates, Stephen B. *Let the Trumpet Sound: The Life of Martin Luther King, Jr.* New York: Harper & Row (1982).

Read More

Adler, David. *A Picture Book of Martin Luther King, Jr.* New York: Holiday House (1990).

de Kay, James. *Meet Martin Luther King, Jr.* New York: Random House (2001).

King, Martin Luther, Jr. *I Have a Dream.* New York: Scholastic (1997).

Levine, Ellen. *If You Lived at the Time of Martin Luther King.* New York: Scholastic (1994).

Marzollo, Jean. *Happy Birthday, Martin Luther King.* New York: Scholastic (1993).

Learn More Online

Visit these Web sites to learn more about Dr. Martin Luther King, Jr.:

seattletimes.nwsource.com/mlk/index.html
www.nps.gov/malu/
www.thekingcenter.org/

Index

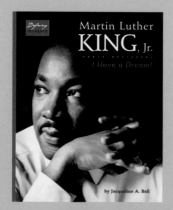

About the Author

JACQUELINE A. BALL has written and produced more than one hundred books for kids and adults. She lives in New York City and Old Lyme, Connecticut.